"To Isaiah, my well-read firstborn. I love you, son."
DD

—

"Beautifully illustrated... theologically strong... and, importantly, kids will love it!"
JIMMY SCROGGINS, Lead Pastor, Family Church, South Florida

"Don't underestimate this children's book. Its message is gigantic."
J.A. MEDDERS, author and pastor

"It's great to be reminded how Jesus is always a far better friend to us than we are to him."
SAM ALLBERRY, author and speaker

"A great resource to teach children about the forgiveness and friendship they can find in Jesus."
DR. MELISSA TUCKER, Associate Professor of Education at Boyce College

"As a parent and a pastor, this is a message I constantly want to keep before my children and the congregation I serve. Jesus is a friend of sinners. Even when we fail, his love doesn't."
BRYAN "BRAILLE" WINCHESTER, recording artist known as Braille

"Another favorite to add to the collection."
JANE WATKINS, Director of Mentoring at Growing Young Disciples

"Dan DeWitt makes big truths about Jesus clear and compelling. I love this book!"
BARBARA REAOCH, author of *A Jesus Christmas* and *A Jesus Easter*

"My lifelong love of reading began with books like this one."
KAREN SWALLOW PRIOR, author of *On Reading Well: Finding the Good Life through Great Books;* and *Booked: Literature in the Soul of Me*

"This book takes you on an uplifting journey."
DR. CRYSTAL K. GRAY, clinical psychologist and co-founder of Clear Sight Music

The Friend Who Forgives
© Dan DeWitt / Catalina Echeverri 2018.
Reprinted 2019, 2020 (twice), 2021 (three times), 2022, 2023 (twice).

Illustrated by Catalina Echeverri | Design & Art Direction by André Parker

'The Good Book For Children' is an imprint of The Good Book Company Ltd
thegoodbook.com | thegoodbook.co.uk | thegoodbook.com.au | thegoodbook.co.nz | thegoodbook.co.in

ISBN: 9781784983024 | JOB-007338 | Printed in India

thegoodbook
for children

THE FRIEND WHO FORGIVES

DAN DEWITT

CATALINA ECHEVERRI

A TRUE STORY ABOUT how PETER FAILED and JESUS FORGAVE

A long time ago there was a man named Peter
who was best friends with Jesus.

Peter was a fisherman.
He was strong and brave. But...

He often said the wrong thing.

Do you ever talk before you think?
That's what Peter did—
        again, and again, and again.

Peter loved fish! In fact, one day he
and Jesus had fish for breakfast.

Fish for breakfast???
        ...That's weird!

But we will save that part
of the story until the end.

On the day when Jesus first called
Peter to follow him, can you guess
what Peter was doing?

That's right.
Peter was fishing.

"Follow me, and I will make you a fisher of men," Jesus told him.

Can you imagine that? Peter fishing for men?

Jesus explained that, just as Peter liked to search for fish, Jesus had come to search for people who needed forgiveness.

Peter loved being friends with Jesus.
He saw Jesus do lots of amazing things.

One time, Peter's mother-in-law
was sick.
Jesus healed her.

Another time, Peter was
about to drown in a storm.
Jesus saved him.

Slowly, Peter realized that Jesus was
more than a friend—he was God!
He would never let Peter down.

But sometimes Peter let Jesus down.
Like the time Jesus explained to his friends that
he had to die on the cross but that he would come
back to life to offer forgiveness.

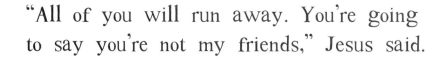

"All of you will run away. You're going
to say you're not my friends," Jesus said.

Peter spoke up right away—
he did that a lot!

I WILL NEVER DO THAT!

Peter said.

But Jesus told him, "Before the rooster crows in the morning, you will say three times that you're not my friend."

"I would never do that.
Jesus is my best friend,"
Peter thought.

When soldiers came to take Jesus to the cross, Peter pulled out his sword to stop them.

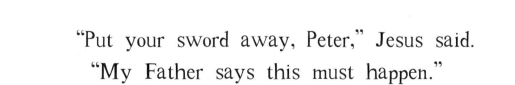

"Put your sword away, Peter," Jesus said. "My Father says this must happen."

Jesus let the soldiers take him to a courtyard to stand trial. Peter followed from far away.

"Aren't you one of Jesus's friends?" a young girl asked as she opened a gate for Peter to enter the courtyard.

What do you think Peter said?

It was a cold night so Peter walked over to a fire where some people were warming themselves.

"Aren't you one of Jesus's friends?" someone asked Peter.

What do you think Peter said?

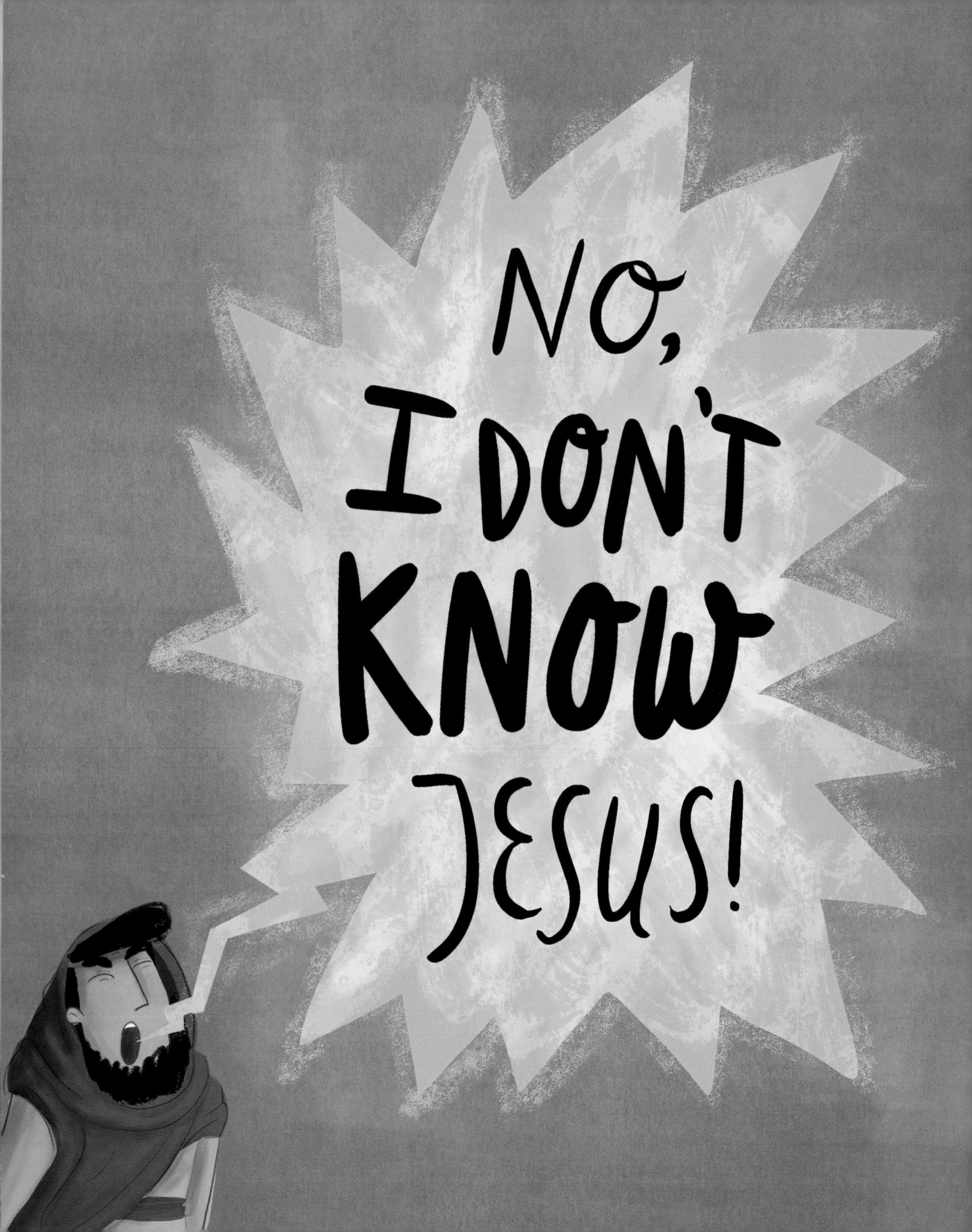
NO, I DON'T KNOW JESUS!

Right then, at that very moment, a rooster crowed.
Jesus turned around and looked straight at Peter.

Then Peter remembered that Jesus had said,

"Before the rooster crows, you will say three times that you are not my friend."

Peter was so sad. He knew he had failed
Jesus again, and again, and again.

He didn't just need to find other
people who needed forgiving.

He needed forgiving too.

Peter felt terrible. He ran out of the courtyard, and he cried, and cried, and cried.

Peter had let his best friend down, and now it was too late because the soldiers had taken Jesus away to be killed.

But Peter didn't stay sad, because Jesus didn't stay dead.

Three days later was the first Easter Sunday, when Jesus came back to life to offer people forgiveness.

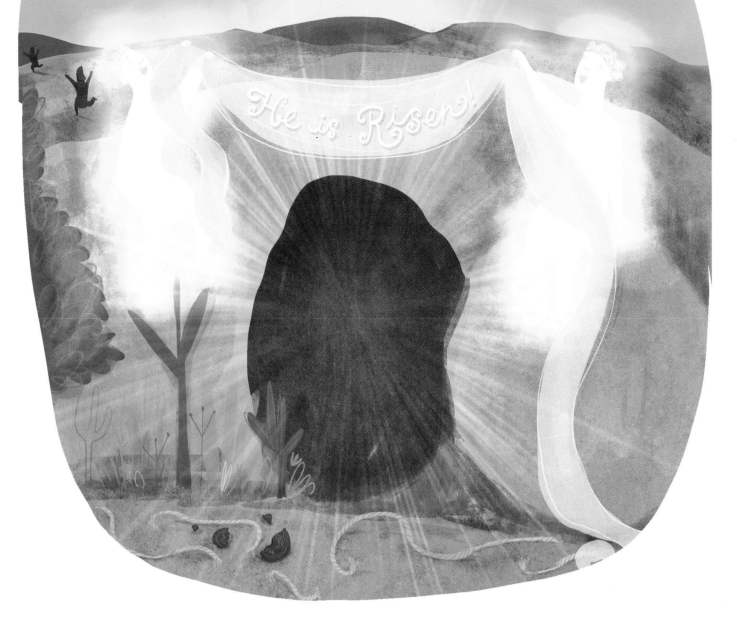

But would he forgive Peter for failing so badly?

One day, Jesus went looking for Peter.
Where do you think Jesus found him?

That's right.

Peter and his friends
were fishing.

Jesus called to them from the beach.

Peter jumped out of the boat into the water,

and rushed to the beach to see Jesus.

And this is where Jesus and Peter
had fish for breakfast.

Fish for breakfast??? That's weird!

Peter was so happy to see Jesus alive,
but would Jesus forgive him? Peter wasn't sure.

Maybe Jesus wouldn't want to talk to him...
Maybe Jesus wouldn't want to be friends with him...

But, yes, Jesus did want to talk to Peter!

And, yes, Jesus did want to forgive Peter! Wow!

And since Peter had said he didn't know Jesus three times, Jesus gave Peter the chance to say three times,

"I love you, Jesus."

That's how Peter became a
forgiven fisher of men!

Peter spent the rest of his life telling people
about his best friend, Jesus.

He told them that if they put
their trust in Jesus, he would
forgive them—
again, and again, and again.

That's because Jesus was Peter's best
friend. He forgave him again, and again,
                              and again!

And if you trust in Jesus, he
will forgive you, too—
     again, and again, and again.

HOW DO WE KNOW
ABOUT THE FRIEND WHO FORGIVES?

The four Gospels—Matthew, Mark, Luke, and John—all tell us about Peter's exciting friendship with Jesus. But then Jesus was arrested—and Peter pretended, three times, that he didn't even know Jesus (Luke 22 v 60-62). Then Jesus was killed on the cross, and it seemed like the end of everything. But Jesus didn't stay dead (Luke 24 v 6)!

The last chapter in John's Gospel tells us that Jesus came to find Peter to forgive him (John 21 v 1-19). Three times, Jesus asked, "Do you love me?" Three times, Peter answered, "Yes, Lord, you know that I love you."

That's how Peter became a forgiven fisher of men. From then on, Peter told other people about Jesus, and how they could be forgiven too—again, and again, and again (Acts 2 v 38; 10 v 43). Peter even wrote part of the Bible for us, so that we can hear him telling us about the friend who forgives too (1 Peter 1 v 18-21; 3 v 18).

Enjoy all of the award-winning
"Tales That Tell The Truth" series: